What
Characteristics of Animals and Plants?

HOUGHTON MIFFLIN HARCOURT

PHOTOGRAPHY CREDITS: COVER ©Barbara Müller-Walter (Jorbasa)/Getty Images; 3 (b) ©Alamy Images; 4 (t) ©Getty Images; 5 (br) ©Getty Images; 6 (tc) ©Stuart Wilson/Photo Researchers, Inc.; 6 (tl) ©Mark C Ross/Fotolia; 6 (tr) ©Enigma/Alamy; 7 (b) ©Klaas Lingbeek- van Kranen/Vetta/Getty Images; 8 (tr) ©Joerg Carstensen/EPA/Corbis; 9 (b) ©Matt Jeppson/Shutterstock; 10 (t) ©Vitaly Titov & Maria Sidelnikova/Shutterstock

Printed in Mexico

ISBN: 978-0-544-07257-2

4 5 6 7 8 9 10 0908 21 20 19 18 17 16 15 14

4500469985 A B C D E F G

Be an Active Reader!

Look at these words.

flower	cone	mammal
pollen	insect	reproduce
seed	fish	metamorphosis
germinate	bird	larva
seedling	amphibian	pupa
life cycle	reptile	nymph

Look for answers to these questions.

What are some plant parts?

What are different plant life cycles?

How can you group animals?

What are some animal coverings?

What are different animal life cycles?

What is metamorphosis?

What are some plant parts?

Roots, stems, leaves, and flowers are all important plant parts. Each part has an important job to do. It helps the plant live and grow!

Often, you cannot see a plant's roots. Most roots grow below ground. A plant's roots are helpful in many ways. A plant's roots take in water and nutrients from the soil. Roots also hold a plant in place and keep it from falling over.

Roots take in water and nutrients from the soil.

Some small animals, like bees, help carry pollen from one flower to another.

A plant's stem brings water and nutrients to the plant's leaves and flowers.

The leaves of a plant have an important job, too. Leaves use water, air, and sunlight to make the plant's food.

A flower helps a plant make new plants. The flower uses a powder called pollen to make seeds. Some seeds grow into new plants.

What are different plant life cycles?

A pumpkin's life begins as a seed. With water and sunlight, seeds germinate, or begin to grow. A seed grows into a seedling, or young plant. The seedling grows into a vine.

Flowers bloom on the vine. The pumpkin forms from a flower. As pumpkins grow, seeds grow inside them. Pumpkin seeds grow into pumpkins. This is the pumpkin's life cycle. A pumpkin's life cycle is the changes in its life. The life cycle repeats over and over.

This pumpkin is fully grown and ready to be picked.

The life cycle of a pine tree starts with a tiny seed.

cone with seeds

young pine tree

adult pine tree

Like a pumpkin, a pine tree begins as a seed. A cone stores seeds. When a cone from the pine tree falls to the ground, seeds fall out. Some seeds grow into trees.

As a young tree grows, it gets bigger. It becomes an adult pine tree. The pine tree produces cones. Then the life cycle begins again!

How can you group animals?

You can group similar animals together. An insect is an animal that has three body parts and six legs. Many insects fly. Bees and ants are insects.

Fish live in water. They get oxygen through their gills. Fish use their fins to swim. Most fish lay eggs.

A bird has feathers and wings. Most birds fly. All birds lay eggs.

Gills and fins allow fish to live in water.

An amphibian has smooth, wet skin. Amphibians lay eggs in water. Their young live in water. As adults, most amphibians live on land. A frog is an amphibian.

Unlike an amphibian, a reptile has dry skin that is covered with scales. Most reptiles lay eggs. Snakes and turtles are reptiles.

Dolphins are mammals.

A mammal has hair or fur. Most female mammals give birth to their young. Young mammals drink milk from their mothers.

What are some animal coverings?

Coverings help animals meet their basic needs. Some animals, such as polar bears, have thick fur. It keeps the bears warm. Some fish have scales. Scales protect their bodies. Birds have feathers that help them fly. Feathers keep birds warm, too.

Some animals use camouflage to hide from predators. Their coverings blend in with their environment.

This animal's covering protects it from predators.

What are different animal life cycles?

Puppies look like their adult parents when they are born.

Animals can reproduce, or have young. Like plant life cycles, animal life cycles repeat.

A bird hatches from an egg and grows. It becomes an adult bird. Then it lays eggs.

An adult dog has puppies. Puppies grow and change. As adults, dogs can have their own young. The life cycle of the dog begins again.

What is metamorphosis?

Some animals go through a series of changes called metamorphosis.

A butterfly begins its life in an egg. A caterpillar, or larva, hatches from the egg. The caterpillar makes a case. Inside the case, the caterpillar changes to a pupa. Then a butterfly emerges.

A nymph, or young grasshopper, hatches from an egg. As the grasshopper grows, it sheds its skin and grows wings.

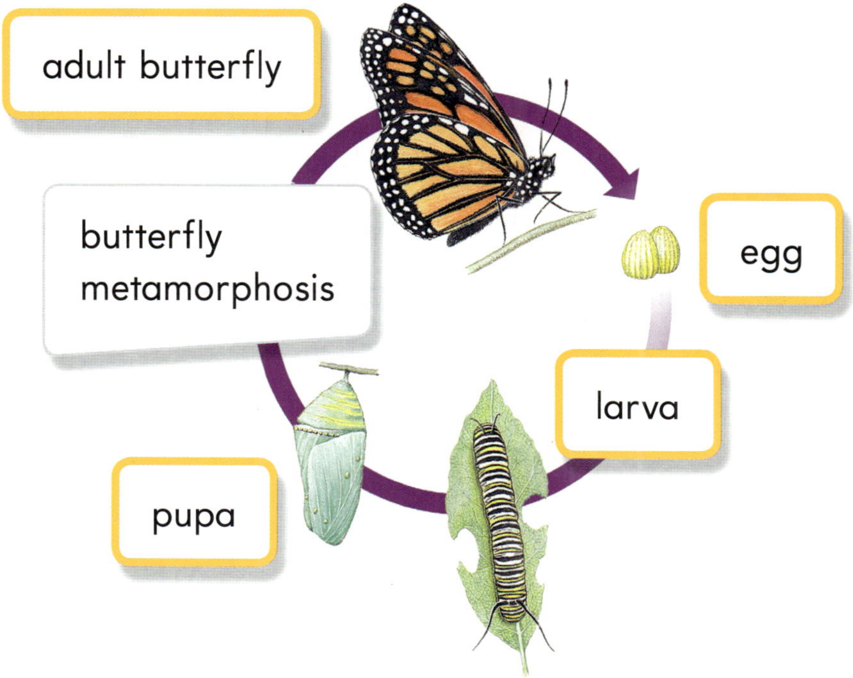

Responding

Compare Animal Characteristics

Choose two animals to research. Investigate each animal's covering, body parts, diet, and life cycle.

Make a Venn Diagram

Draw two large overlapping circles. Write the name of one animal above the left circle. In the circle, record characteristics of the animal. Write the name of another animal above the right circle. In that circle, record characteristics of that animal. In the area where the circles overlap, record characteristics that the animals share.